LOCAL WEATHER

ANDREW SQUITIRO

a **DYNAMO VERLAG** joint.

LOCAL WEATHER

This book is published by **DYNAMO VERLAG**

Capitol Hill, D.C., Echo Park, Los Angeles, Seattle, and St. Louis

Cover design by Caleb True

Printed in the U.S.A.

10 9 8 7 6 5 4 3 2 1 blast off.

DYNAMOVERLAG.com

TABLE OF CONTENTS

LOCAL WEATHER

ANDREW SQUITIRO

LOCAL WEATHER I

There are different names for what air can do to the gulf. An invest, a depression, a cyclone, a hurricane. Invests don't get to be named, only numbered. Invest 90L has a 60% chance of formation by Friday, but formation into… what? It's already circling, an eye in the center.

Sometimes, you can feel the drop in pressure before the collective shrieking of SMS alerts in the cafe. In Missouri, the air turned green. Here, it's different. Like the pulse in your throat when the power surges and the collective din of fans, the refrigerator, and window units power down. When you can hear a roach as he scurries into the new darkness. When the silence reminds you your apartment is haunted, been haunted for years.

There's always a storm in the distance here, flashes of light over the lake and river, just out of reach but not out of sight, always inaudible. They're there every night in the summer, six months of flickering light like a projector sputtering before the movie begins.

Summer is fleeing in the rain, hopscotching over the flooded courtyard to get to my backyard dependency. It's Taking Back Sunday, triple shower days, the darkness of night too short to share them with anyone but you. It's getting so used to the sunrise that we mistake dawn for last call.

What happened to us? I haven't slept with anyone beside you since Mardi Gras, when we both took home tourists and didn't see each other until Ash Wednesday. I came over to do laundry and we made love in the kitchen. Is this how monogamy happens, how commitment begins?

It iced this winter and my pipes burst and I had to give myself sponge baths with bottled Dasani. People called it snow, but it wasn't, it was ice. I don't think it snows anymore, anywhere. 30 is the new 20, and that's how precipitation works when it's hovering around freezing.

I lost power and we couldn't get in touch, but you were gone for it anyway, like you always are, back home for winter like a homesick undergrad. I worry each time you leave that you'll stay there, that you'll give in to your parents, the comfort of your hometown. I worry how happy you are here.

It's so quiet in the French Quarter now that it makes me uneasy, like the world forgot about us, and everyone was mistaken to visit such a city in the first place. It floods each time it storms now, and it storms daily. I saw a current down Esplanade during the last one, tree limbs rushing toward the river, tiny white peaks in the water.

It's tempting to wish for things to stay like this forever, the impossible heat acting as gatekeeper, only letting in the people willing to put up with it, or the ones who can't bear to leave the only home they've known. I'm speaking from privilege here, of course.

In which category do you fall? Close your eyes and picture another city and tell me it isn't hell. Portland, Oakland, New York? A stray dart's landing, somewhere in the Midwest?

I can't picture myself anywhere but right here, right now. I haven't thought of the future in years, and how could I when I can't even picture the end of summer, just an endless string of August days, 40, 50, 60, 100.

I can only picture what I see, and right now it's you in this morning, wet with dew and sweat, the ceiling fan on high. Your back curling away from my stomach and its heat, your phone in your hands.

LOCAL WEATHER II

When the storm misses us, life begins again awkwardly. Like the colliding noses of a bungled first kiss, there's an understanding that this will happen again soon, for real this time. Except kisses are exciting, and storms are disastrous.

But I still find myself excited for bad weather. Excited for the kiss that shouldn't happen, yet know it will. Excited because it will be hotter, better, sexier than the normal mashing of lips. Two people in love are greater than the sum of their parts, but if you replace "in love" with "in an affair," the adage still holds water. The only difference is one is healthy, and the other is destructive.

I'm always trying to find a healthy outlet for my body's yearning toward self-destruction. But you can't replace cigarettes with baking, or all-night benders with morning jogs. The math doesn't work. And there are so few things in this world to enjoy, that rejecting affection comes off forced.

This is how I rationalize always ending up here, a two-hundred-year storm beating down on your air conditioner, the racket so loud we use our mouths for touch instead of speech. The disaster of me in your bedroom, a pint of warm gin between us, your boyfriend on voicemail.

And then the letdown. Last year, when they set the curfew for 6:00PM, I waited in my room until then and went for a walk. Everyone in my neighborhood went for a walk. The streets were cluttered with spontaneous dog-walkers, people on porches, punks on the neutral ground, unaware of the sudden, parish-wide ordinance, the winds in the gulf.

I walked past a bar boarded up, "WE ARE OPEN — FUCK OFF NATE" spray-painted on the plywood. Nate was a hurricane that never came, its western arm dissolving on landfall in the miles of wetlands between us and the ocean.

I wonder how long they waited until taking out the screwdriver and removing the boards. Until admitting, no, it's not coming, and resigning themselves to another slow, summer weekend, a few tips from regulars in place whatever can happen when you lock a bunch of strangers inside a well-stocked bar.

You asked me this weekend if I've ever loved anyone, and I said of course. I've been in four relationships, each neatly divided into one year of harmony, one year of trying to make it work. Bricks crumbling while we wipe the red dust from the sheets. Being asked, why do you like me, being unable to answer.

No, you said. If you love someone, you stay with them forever. But isn't that trite? Doesn't that negate independence, agency? Does love begin where the self ends? And really, which means are necessary, and for what end? I think of this quote, shakily attributed to Harvey Milk:

Go after her. Fuck, don't sit there and wait for her to call. Go after her because that's what you should do if you love someone, don't wait for them to give you a sign because it might never come. Don't let people happen to you, don't let me happen to you, or her, she's not a fucking television show or tornado.

I'm always disappointed and embarrassed by the difference between real life and television. As much as this quote rails against fantasy, it's still fantasy in itself. I've flown to Oregon, driven Iowa in an instant, put my fist through a window in a moment of private, hopefully profound rage.

None of it mattered. You can't change someone, and if you could, what would be the point? There's a finer line than we'd like to admit between desire for a commodity and desire for the beloved.

There's also a line between drama and fantasy, romance and real life. A decade-long partnership is built upon a hundred grocery runs for every teary, heartfelt gesture. Right?

When Obama is asked about his career and successes, he answers, It's about the work. You have to like the work. But what if you don't? Are those of us like me destined for perpetual heartache — all because we can't deal with the grocery runs, dinners, the endless oil leak of living for more than one?

It's embarrassing, but the sameness scares me more than another strain, fissure, crack in the stained glass of my heart.

But when does heartache itself become monotonous? The friends I know who weather the storm are the ones who are sick of evacuating. They stay not for the drama, but to avoid the letdown of nothing happening, again.

They can see it a mile away. The long awkward drive back, air-conditioning on high. Cars broken-down on the shoulder, overheated in the gridlock. Death by monotony and the long, summer heat

But one day, the storm will hit. And those same friends will say it won't, but it will. And God-willing, I'll be here too. Drinking whisky on the front porch with them because the power's out, will be for weeks, and it's cooler outside than in.

LOCAL WEATHER III

It's been cooler lately. Not in New Orleans, but in New Jersey, where I've been teaching teenagers for the past few weeks. Whenever I am someplace new, it's hard to convince myself that I've actually travelled, that I've traversed some real distance, and that this landscape isn't some sort of virtual manifestation, a simulation, the road following the car instead of the wheels turning.

A week ago, I met a girl in D.C. who said she manifested my appearance in her life. Something about vibration, energy, an aura around me. She stayed in a top-floor penthouse in Kalorama Heights with dwindling Hennessy and a girlfriend she hadn't left yet. She told me that everything happens for a reason.

I don't believe in the supernatural, but I do like it when people notice me, when someone spots me with a look in a crowd that says, you, I see you, and for a moment, I don't feel so alien anymore.

When we were kids, my sister was taken to the forest and I was taken to the fields, the wide open prairies of Kansas where a white woman with land told me I had powers that were different from most people, and that it was my choice to use these powers for good, for evil, or to ignore them altogether.

We walked through the labyrinth she scythed in her cornfield and we talked to the victims of 9/11 in the center, and afterward, she measured how much our auras had grown with dousing rods, and I was proud that mine had grown the most. She had to cross the highway behind her house until the rods crossed, and my aura was no longer measurable.

This was seventeen years ago — a lifetime to some — and here I am, trying to convince one of my students, a boy from far away, that it's safe to go to sleep here. We go for a walk and I talk about the deer, the fireflies, anything to distract him from his rapid heartbeat and wild thoughts, a feeling I've known well, but thankfully outgrown.

Here in what I call the north, I sleep with the windows open and the A/C off, letting the dew mix with my sweat. It's easy to sleep like this when you need to wake up at 7:00AM, when the sun is only a source of light instead of heat, when the air is still cool with the night.

When he goes to bed I think of my own boy, the boy in New Orleans, who it's taken me six months to still not understand. The boy who makes me feel like a teenager myself — our staccato touches and coded language, a constant negotiation of unspoken boundaries, unspoken because the language is still so new to us.

I text him but he doesn't respond until I've already fallen asleep, and when I wake up I read his messages and they're cute, they make me smile, but I wonder why I even have his number.

There are parts of me that are so hard to consciously change, but change so easily with the rain, the scenery, the simple falling of the sun. The person I am at night is so different than the one I am at noon in New Jersey, 10:00PM in Venice, 3:00AM on I-10. I wonder how common the threads are really. Creator and destroyer, protector and preserver. It can get exhausting.

The lover and the thief, the fool and the genius. The boy who will stay up and smoke cigarettes with you until the sun rises, because you say you've never stayed up that late before. The adulterer, the anarchist. The boy psychic who rejected his powers just to feel normal. The boy who was lied to by low-grade cultists.

I want so desperately to sew all these parts of myself into a complete person, but I'm running out of thread. Every first kiss, new rejection, old addiction is another patch I need to stitch in. I'm worried that one day I'll run out of thread completely — that I'll be left with all these threadbare patches, a collection of lives unfinished, a pile of scraps that doesn't add up to very much at all.

LOCAL WEATHER IV

Back to the heat, back to the swamp. Back to the long days of mopping sweat from my brow, waiting out storms in crowded cafes, the dullness and deluge of summer.

If you follow the balconies, you can get from point to point in the quarter unscathed from the downpour. You just need patience and cunning to chart your way through dry. The garbage bag ponchos work well to identify the tourists, if it weren't easy enough already.

I went to sleep in rain and woke up in rain, the water delaying my only plans for the day— laundry in the quarter. By the time I would make it to her shop, Miss Dinah will have claimed every machine for herself, say she didn't think anyone would be coming to her today.

Sometimes, shortcuts can be scenic instead of short. In Columbia, I'd take Rock Creek Road, a woodland rollercoaster that I'd fly through whenever I could, downshifting on the turns in my '99 Civic.

Years later, we drove through there again. Slowly, this time. My '95 ranger creeping through the turns because we were drunk and you were nauseous, and I didn't mind prolonging your company.

You asked me to pull over and we got out and laid on the shoulder, and the sky was so thick with stars it looked like a torn off bandage. You puked on the asphalt and we didn't kiss anymore, but I still held you, and your breathing got easier.

We talked about how weird it was to be back in Missouri, and you punched me for cheating on you when we first met, back when our relationship was still fresh and had the most potential. The only time we shared the same city, a time I desperately regret wasting.

It wasn't cheating, but I didn't care enough to argue. I let you keep hitting me and was surprised you still thought of me in New York. For better or worse, I'm not one to turn away affection — especially when it's strong enough to raise voices or put a fist into drywall. It's not a trait I'm proud of.

I was raised thinking that when you loved someone enough, that's how you showed it — in violent outbursts of dishes and chairs, screaming until your throat turned raw. Once, I told my mom to go fuck herself, then threw a glass from the porch into the street. Even at fifteen, I knew this to be more preferable to her than a calm tone and neutral expression, a pillow in a thunderstorm. To speak softly was to display indifference.

Now that I know this part of myself, it's easier to control. I still have a soft spot for the violent and dramatic — what some would call passion. It's an issue I'm working on, but I'll have the scars from the shattered mirrors, walls, and car windows forever. The things I've broken.

I hate the notion that we're all broken, because it's so defeatist, so absolving. If every parent is a bad one, then how can I hold mine accountable, why should I change? I hate working on my issues, would rather half-believe that the knowledge of my issues is enough, that to know the devil is to disarm him, but that's not how it works. You need to confront him.

You need the humility to pick up the pieces and do something productive with them to keep the devil away, even if you know he'll always be at the door. I think often of how easy it'd be to destroy my life forever. A credit card, a handle, a carton of smokes. You can get it all at one store. It's amazing anyone is sane at all.

In this long morning of storms and no power, I have nothing to do but stay in bed and be hungover. The air is thick and the rain on the air-conditioner sounds like the pitter patter of rifle fire.

I'm drawn to rain for the same reason I'm drawn to prayer and fasting — it forces humility. There's something humble in the ridiculousness of kneeling at your bedside, in showing up to the party soaking wet.

If I were a better man today, I'd put on clothes and clean the house, do the dishes, call my folks. I'd do something with the day and these four-hundred square feet that I get to call mine. Make use of this time in my life without a spouse, child, career — any sort of actual anchor or chain.

But my head hurts, I'm hungry, and I may throw up as soon as my feet touch the tile. So I don't.

Instead, I'll waste the day looking through my phone, listening to the rain. I've engineered everything in my life up to this point to allow me the freedom necessary to stay inside, if I choose.

If I were a better man, I wouldn't have the choice.

LOCAL WEATHER V

The weather is gorgeous but I can't stop sleeping nine, ten, eleven hours straight through the morning. When I leave my house and go into the garden, it's already nightfall. Did it rain at some point?

4:00PM surprises me. The streets are already clogged with people getting home, anxious to sleep through the day I've barely begun. They'll go to sleep before midnight and wake up with an alarm. They'll let the dogs out, take the kids to school, themselves to work. I have absolutely no idea what it's like to live like this.

We were together for two years, been apart almost the same, but yesterday on the phone you agreed that it could've been yesterday that I was leaving for work, kissing your sleeping body, putting on my belt and boots on the porch. The built habits of an expired life.

Sometimes, I wouldn't realize I'd wakened you. You'd appear on the porch in a shroud of quilts and sheets and kiss me there and watch me leave.

I remember a lot about us asleep. Chewing melatonin together. Listening to your roommates have sex. The innate, instinctual way you'd reach for me, even while unconscious. I'll never get over that — the way your arm wanted me as natural as a mouth wants water.

But really, I spent more time next to you asleep than awake. It's fitting that, after righting myself from our fall, I spend more time now with the night than the day. My work requires it, and also — the languid winter sun. It's like I've replaced your absence by filling the darkness — with work, alcohol, the occasional other person. It doesn't matter.

I didn't expect this, but I asked for it. I like where I am, but I do sometimes wish you were still here. Even if we were uncomfortable, unstable, what some told me toxic. Several times a friend would pull me aside to say seriously, "I'm worried about you Andrew." I was too, but I always had faith we would find a way forward, even if that faith were bad.

It doesn't rain so much anymore, just blows a cold air gently through every gash in my shutters and french doors. I want to know I still affect you somehow. There's folklore in Japan that says, if you love someone unreachable — be it a lover or a deceased — they'll infect you. Their spirit will take the body of a fox and they'll enter you, through your eyelids or nipples, in the dead of night. I always liked that the dead and the former lover were one in the same. It seems true.

Sometimes I'd know before you called that you weren't showing up. We fell into each other so quick, that of course there are still scars. It's not the length of a love, but the ferocity, and we were nothing if not ferocious. I don't see how there wouldn't be initials carved into your heart like mine.

You always reminded me that what was yours was mine, and vice versa. When you were stressed, you wanted me stressed too. And that went the same with your body — you gave yourself to me, trusted me so quickly.

It was like someone snapped their fingers, and we were two stems of the same flower. But we weren't.

We were more kudzu than orchid, and I never heard the snap.

We were still separate, two people with their own ethereal, unpredictable wiles. And you saw that. I wish I could've merged into you the way you merged into me, be two halves of the same whole, but that's something I'll never be able to do. I will be always be my own thing.

LOCAL WEATHER VI

What do you do while the world ends? It's sixty degrees in winter, so I'm standing outside at midnight, sharing a cigarette, wearing a jacket that's mostly for show. I'm in Kansas City this week, and a new friend tells me I'm lucky I chose now to visit, because the weather's so nice. The apocalypse shouldn't be so pleasant, but it is. It's divine.

The weather is nice everywhere this time of year. If you're in North America and reading this, it could easily be sixty degrees wherever you are, yet we know it shouldn't be. The reason it's sixty degrees is because our climate is being actively and violently destroyed every second, yet the people with the power to change that aren't doing much.

Every 100 minutes, a football field of Louisiana coastline disappears. Just vanishes into the ocean. And despite all that oil money, no one here is rich. We are one of poorest states in the union. Yet, who is profiting from the vanishing of our state? "Exxon alone, one company, has 7% of the carbon in its reserves necessary to take us past [the] red line" that destroys the planet irreversibly. These companies should be absolved immediately, but they won't be. It's their oil, and they deserve a profit.

And it's not just the changing climate. Our schools are striated by greed, jealousy, and the rarely discussed fear of white parents sending their children to predominantly black schools.

People are dying everyday from silly, preventable things: illnesses with cures, overdose, gun violence, the unusual severity and frequency of natural disasters. In every major American city, you will probably pass by a person collapsed on the sidewalk if you go for a walk downtown.

The two top-selling drugs on the U.S. market are for an antidepressant and a heart disease medication — which of course is caused by obesity, which of course is caused by a sedentary, unhealthy, consumerist society that smugly discourages anything that is natural or free.

And because of all this, more and more carbon is released, and the ice caps keep melting, and the earth gets a little warmer than usual.

Back in New Orleans, I fixed up my bike and rode it out to the levee, watched the sunset, called a friend. There was a breeze and the scent of winter in the air, but still, a jacket would've been superfluous. It was gorgeous outside.

Living below sea level, near the ocean, surrounded by gas refineries and a precariously-placed nuclear reactor, it's hard to put the impending disaster in the back of your mind. It's not something we like to discuss with outsiders (and I'm still a bit fresh to use the pronoun we), but the fact remains, this place won't exist a hundred years from now.

Honestly, it might not make it twenty. It doesn't have to be like this, there are things we could be doing, but let's be real. We can recycle bicycle tires and ban plastic bags, but it's not people that pollute, it's corporations and militaries. And they're not going to stop.

Everyone I know is tired and broken-hearted because the apocalypse is currently happening, and not in a sexy, The Walking Dead type of way. Our evil is banal. There is still slavery in the world — slavery that I benefit from — and actively ongoing genocides on multiple continents, yet it's easier somehow to sympathize with 20th century Jews than the 21st century Rohingya, or the children who make my clothes and cellphone. No one cares.

Not to mention the troubles at home, in the United States. There is so much that is wrong with the world it's a wonder that only one in six Americans are actively taking antidepressants. Andrea Gibson is right when she asks, "Do we really believe our need for Prozac / has nothing to do with Baghdad?" And I don't mean to vilify those on any sort of medication — I'm glad it exists. Xanax is in my medicine cabinet.

But it's hard not to imagine why one would be depressed, and I highly doubt it's a society-wide chemical imbalance. We are all depressed because we have very good reasons to be depressed — all you have to do is look under the veil and see the awful way we treat one another, the way our society treats women and minorities, the way our species treats the earth.

It's so fucking banal, but in 2004, 25% of Americans said they had no one they could confide in. It doesn't seem like there's a middle-ground between playing cornhole at the brewery on Friday and overdosing on Sunday. On Tinder, it really seems like Netflix and sleep are our number one hobbies. Going out is a chore to most. Our attention spans are shot. Teenagers would rather call an uber than cruise around town.

I can't decide whether it's good or not to look under the veil. If I'm sad, I listen to a sad song. If I'm happy, I like to laugh and shout. But what should I do in winter, when it's seventy degrees, and I'm shirtless in the garden, working on my bike?

Do I write my congressman, buy some reusable grocery bags off Amazon, be better about turning off the lights before leaving? Or do I enjoy the day, and believe that my knowledge of the issue is enough? I don't know, I have no clue. I feel culpable, yet paralyzed.

If I were sick, I'd see a doctor. Listen well. Call my mom from the parking lot when I'm finished. But the world is sick and no one cares. It's dying right in front of me, every day, despite the gorgeous weather and my comfortable, American lifestyle. The world is ending and no one's going to stop it.

LOCAL WEATHER VII

The progression from new love to companionship never goes easily for me. The transition from land to water, shore to sea. You have to give me time alone in the evenings. I have to give you time during the day to work.

We have to let each other do the things that make us who we are, because if we don't, then we wouldn't be distinct people anymore. We'd just be two bodies, dully writhing in my damp apartment. That wouldn't be interesting.

If we always felt the way we first felt about each other, we'd never get anything done. New love needs to end, for the sake of everything else.

Summer gets all the credit for its humidity, but in the winter, the air is so wet, my walls weep with sweat. My sheets are damp. The floor is so soaked I could wipe it with a dry rag and drink from the excess. I could sustain myself for years on the scraps of love you've given me. And I do. You're never around, but I answer your calls.

Last night, I drove the flyover around the Superdome and the fog was so thick, I couldn't see the buildings that I remembered to be there. I have so many issues — people have so many issues. The tired advice is to fix yourself before imposing your love on someone else, but I'm growing skeptical of that thinking.

As Brandy Jensen writes in her Ask a Fuck Up column, people (specifically men) need to "grow the fuck up" and be there for people while being there for themselves. I'm sure some would disagree, find her advice problematic. I'm sure some would find my adherence to her advice even more problematic. I don't know, I'm bad at knowing how others want me to be.

There are some things I need to admit I have no control over: the rising tide, the way I was raised, the children dying in cages on our own soil. The emotions of other people — to an extent, of course.

I have a list of people to apologize to that'd put any ninth-stepper to shame. "First be reconciled to your brother, and then come and offer your gift" (Mt. 5:24). Should I patch things up with my last lover before finding someone else? Should I volunteer at the food bank before going to the border?

No matter what anyone does, you can pick it apart and point out an endless amount of absurdity and bias.

Toward the end of the novel, Annihilation, the biologist finds herself gazing at the dead body of her colleague and thinking about her husband to whom she was growing distant before his disappearance:

The arguing came later, when it became real to me. But never pleading. I never begged him to stay. I couldn't do that. Perhaps he even thought that going away would save our marriage, that somehow it would bring us closer together. I don't know. I have no clue. Some things I will never be good at.

The last few lines kill me. There are so many things I feel this way toward. I could live in my bathroom, washing my hands in perpetuity. And I should, to an extent.

I know I'm not God, I know I can't control everything, especially other people. I know it isn't fair to try.

But there has to be a middle ground, and I think the middle ground is actually what defines us as people. It's our entirety. The things we feel in control over versus the things we feel powerless toward.

What do you feel culpable toward? Are you actually? Who's responsible, who's in charge? In this light, the Serenity Prayer is more parable than prayer.

I rarely see the point in ending things with someone completely. Our lives are so complicated and meandering, love so difficult to come by, acceptance even rarer, that I find it natural to stay in contact. To say hi when I'm around. To be lenient when it comes to the jobs, locales. The problems that separate us intermittently. The current, past, and future lovers.

What's it matter that you found a job on the coast, went there, met a different guy to keep you company? He doesn't love you the way I love you — and you love the way I love you. The ways I'm different and the ways you're different when you're around me.

I'm not special, this is just a phenomenon of love. And life is so banal and violent, I can't really afford to ignore any positive phenomena at all.

The air is wet and I want to be with you, and I hate how meaningless and random it is that sometimes I can contact you, and sometimes I can't. How childish I feel, waiting for you to break up with him and reach out. On-demand Andrew.

But this is who I am and it'd feel fake of me to change. Call me when you're single again. I'll be here.

LOCAL WEATHER VIII

They leave the park open up past dark when there's a show at the theater, and tonight there was an Alvin Ailey performance. It was my idea to go initially, but my friend persuaded me away from backing out of the show last minute. We chose to walk over bike and I'm so glad we did — it's the last scraps of our springtime here, before another vast expanse of the near-infinite summer, and it was nice to indulge in the early evening air, before I forget its decadence.

Everyone was dressed up — New Orleanians dress well when the occasion suggests an opportunity — the coats and long dresses gently lit by the early street lamps and fading light of day. Something about events like these give me confidence in the future.

Maybe all this is the orchestra on the Titanic, maybe I'm naive, but the fact that people will actually buy tickets, dress up, and show up to a night at least partially divorced from Netflix and alcohol gives me hope. Distracts me from the reality that the world is rapidly ending.

But it is. I will always have faith in the apocalypse and doubt in the divine. I wish I could change those things within me, but it seems as hardwired as my brown hair and right handed dominance. But the small things — a ballet on a warm spring night, a hot shower in the cold, the color the air takes when it rains but the sun is still out, these give me faith…

in something? A glint, a glimmer? Is faith just another word for appreciation?

It's not an original thought — that nice things are nice — but there's more depth than that. In these days when the basic tenants of humanity are so smugly dismissed, you take what you get. The devil is winning but he's weaker when I'm with you.

Yesterday I spent the day watching my friends' toddler while they worked, and I won't say that he changed my whole perspective on things, but the world I walked was different. It was mostly in the way people treated me — the reason I was stressed, overwhelmed, and so on was manifest in my arms while I tried to navigate a life no longer familiar. The laundromat, the sandwich shop, it was all so much more difficult than I'm used to. But people were nice about it.

They could see me struggling and helped as much as they could. They handed me napkins so I didn't have to get up, made funny faces at him, told me how good I was doing. And that night, I went to the ballet with my friend, with tickets I bought beforehand, and ran into so many people I knew while I was there.

It was Friday, and everyone was happy. We came to see something beautiful together and we did. But we were celebrating something else, too — another week in the history books, another week stolen from the terminal world.

LOCAL WEATHER IX

The drive home is quicker than the drive there — the ticker tape of trees and cars isn't new, so I've stopped paying attention. I'm too used to the terrain, the thoughts, the things that trouble me. Your hair on my neck, my head on your chest. The way I speed through things now that we know each other, how this always happens, and it's so typical. Go slow, she and I both implore.

There's this poem by Li-Young Lee, "The Undressing," that begins with the speaker and beloved in bed, in the space before foreplay:

Listen, she says.

I'm listening, I answer

and kiss her chin.

Obviously, you're not, she says.

And the poem continues from there, the speaker tying to make love to his beloved, her, patiently resisting, trying to explain to a him a deeper thing about the universe, while he ignores and undresses her. What happens when we typecast a person, a thing, a scenery? This is something I've been working on. Letting people be themselves, speak for themselves.

To be friends with someone requires a certain suspension of disbelief. To be lovers, even more. But to be partners? I don't see how other people do it. Similar to claiming a religion, claiming a partner for life seems like the healthy choice, but an impossible one. What room is there for doubt, skepticism, a healthy, academic outlook on the world?

Do I only value skepticism because it's all I've known? Is there an actual virtue behind looking at the abundant miracle of life and saying — prove it.

It's getting hot now, and I'm packing my things mentally because it's too soon to actually get the luggage out before I take off for the summer. I'm leaving for a cooler climate, a breeze in the trees, cool ground. An endless forest to the replace the endless summer this close to the gulf.

It's very easy to get trapped in the endlessness that is New Orleans between May and October. Staying up too late to avoid the heat, sleeping through the day, the deafening air conditioner — or the stale and humid heat, a heat that works similarly to deafen me. And how do you fill something that's constantly draining? Work, then the bar. The bar, then work. I'm trying to avoid all this.

I'm trying to avoid the road I've traveled for so long I've forgotten to look out the window. I want attention, newness, a steady drip of sincerity. I think if I give this to the world, I might receive it in return. I'd like to add something to my world rather than fail in my restraint. I don't have faith in any of this, but I'm willing to try.

LOCAL WEATHER X

The first storm of summer came on Mother's Day last week. It flooded my and everyone else's car on my block. I'd just finished cleaning all the mold out of my closet when the thunder first hit, mopped the thin film of black from the tiles underneath my bed and couch.

I'm afraid mold will remain a constant in my life here, especially in my garden level apartment. The frogs like it, the plants like it, and every week, I do what would otherwise be a deep-clean in any other place I've lived.

Now, there's a faint smell of mildew everywhere I go. There's a dampness to my sheets. If I leave my home for the weekend, when I return, there's a wide, sheer splatter of pink spores over my bathtub and shower curtain. What happened while I was gone? Who did this? Would they rather I stay gone?

I've been thinking lately on the consciousness of things not provably conscious. The way a plant reaches toward the light, how water moves down a hill, how electricity always finds the shortest path between two points. It's scary, isn't it? The diagram of an atom compared to our solar system. And this is just what's simple — if I think too long on the quantum level, I get terrified.

When the basil in my front yard has had too much sun, the leaves will wilt to decrease their surface area. To me, that's will — a decision made, but by who? Is it really so different from a sweating forehead, a dry mouth when thirsty? Our desire for others? And if it isn't, can we then call this instinct?

And if the living world has instinct, what does that mean? Can it get sick, become deranged? Does it have thoughts that precede action? Feeling? When the bacteria conquers the white blood cell, is it happy? Does it feel rewarded?

It's enough to give me chills. To think of the mold, the thunder, the vines all as living things — alive with decisions and impulse. It gives me a different appreciation for the natural world. The frogs croaking before it rains, the cicadas just before sunset. There is so much that is unknowable in the world.

There's a line from the book, Annihilation, "Some questions will ruin you if you are denied the answer long enough." I often feel like the unknown will ruin me, or at least my obsession with it, my inability to accept something or someone completely.

I can't say how many nights I've wasted on you, harassing myself with what I'll never know. Your thoughts when I'm not around, what you think of me, how much you're willing to give. You are a deep, dark canyon, and I get lost in you so easy, but is this really what I want? Is it possible for me to not?

LOCAL WEATHER XI

I've been thinking lately about the small choices I've made that, without intention, have built a life for myself. I don't have many commitments — a few hobbies, an activist group, work, and then my friends. No spouse, no kids (I don't even remember when I had to start saying that). No grad school, no dad in the nursing home. No lagging shackle of the thirty-year mortgage.

But my few friends and commitments are enough to fill the days to the point I say no more than yes. To the point that weeks turn into seasons, and I'm left dragging my winter clothes out of the closet before I ever made it to the pool.

These thoughts are coming from my new job that's shifted my working hours from evening til dawn to sunrise to 5:00PM. The people here speak in years. There are wedding rings and kids around. Everyone's clothes are freshly laundered, their hair washed. No one curses.

I take heart in the fact that I can still jump ship at any moment. It's something I think of often, and very regularly dream about. I have a friend who lives off the railroad and kindness of strangers — her only permanent decision being that she's opted out of permanence. And even though I've never used it, there's both a very literal and also metaphorical bug-out bag stashed in my entryway, ready to go at the first sign of permanence.

Yet, that's not how it happens. I used to imagine permanence as a sort of neo-noir grim reaper, stalking me slowly through the shadows of dive bars and other people's apartments, ready to pounce at any moment and saddle me with a bundle of banal, undue burdens.

But it didn't happen that way. Instead, I said yes to things. It's not because I wish to be successful, it's simple inertia — the gradual stacking of obligations from chess club to the pool team, my socialist group, my work and writing.

The calendar app on my phone binds me to all these simple things I agreed to do once, in the moment, without much thought really put into it. And then I find myself simply driving around the city every day at 7:00 and 5:00, 7:00 again and then, hopefully for the last time, home by 10:00.

And if I don't do anything to change, if I don't add or subtract anything, my Wednesday nights will look the same ten, twenty, thirty years from now. It's not a bad thing, just strange.

Strange also in that, this is how a lot of folks spend their lives too. Driving from one place to the next, seeing the people they agreed to see. There's no great drama around the bend. The milestones have, for the most part, disappeared into the realm of photo albums. I imagine that one day, even the hurricanes and industrial disasters will start to blend together.

I don't know what I was expecting, but it surely wasn't this.

The weather is great now, and it's even better because it's deserved. We suffered through the eternal summer to get this — a handful of months where you can dress how you please, get a chill on your cheek, hold someone close without sticking together. It's nice. We earned it.

A pastor would tell me I earned this life too, just as I earned this nice weather, but I don't think I did. Inertia earned it for me. I simply said sure. And I like having things to do. It keeps me out of the house — the place I always want to be at if I'm not there, but don't really ever enjoy. I don't build memories there.

I used to think that memories were built in trial and turmoil, and they are, but they aren't relegated to that. There are memories available also in the day-to-dayness of things.

I don't totally believe this yet, but I really hope it to be true. And coming back to the photo album, I hope to look at it as Eliot does, in "East Coker,"

There is a time for the evening under starlight,

A time for the evening under lamplight

(The evening with the photograph album).

Love is most nearly itself

When here and now cease to matter.

I think this is the way you build a life. I think we're meant to fill the hours with other people and things, letting our evenings under the stars add to our evenings at home, with the photo album.

Yet, that's also what's so cruel. Once you add all this up — you don't even notice the time when it passes, and there isn't any to left to enjoy it in reminiscence. I'm still trying to reconcile this.

I'm scared of death, but what scares me more is the way it will creep up on me, as simple as January stalks December. I'm scared that my eyes will shut before I've seen everything I'm meant to. I'm scared that I know this all, yet there's nothing I can do to stop it.

LOCAL WEATHER XII

A few hours after sunset, the fog rolls in off the river and hangs over the streets until morning, when the winter sun rises dully to burn it all off, like a pot left on low boil. The steam rises from the lawns and neutral ground, the gardens, even the potted plants in my court yard.

I've held my hand over the steam a few times and, I wouldn't call it hot, but it's warm — warmer than anything else that time of morning.

These long winter nights are good for me because they encourage staying in, or staying out and by myself. It's good for me to be alone and comfortable doing so. And this time of year, it's not weird to be alone in the fog — because so is everything else. I'm speaking of pure visibility here, but also, the weather is affectual. When the fog comes in off the lake and the river, people don't linger in it long.

My photography professor, sick of pictures of cliche benches under a streetlamp, would say, "Night isn't a subject, it's a condition" (I think he was quoting someone else, too). That is to say, Don't take a picture of the night, take a picture of what the night does to you. What the night does to us. It is a condition — an affect.

Just like the night — there are things in the world more powerful than we understand. It's commonly accepted that, if a random person were dropped somewhere in the middle of the woods — be it the

Ozarks or the Amazon — that person would be in serious danger. But of what?

It doesn't matter. Hours in the woods without preparation is dangerous. And I don't think it's just our modern condition that makes it so. Ancient cultures feared the woods just as we do.

When people disappear and are then recovered from the woods, many are unable to say what happened before they were found. It's true. They can't recall the hours between when they were lost and when they were found — or if they can, it's vague and limited.

What's more — the lost walk in circles, strip down when they're frostbitten, hide when they hear rescuers calling them by name. People are very bad at being found. Being in the woods alters something in us and our understanding of reality.

Likewise, the fog that hangs over our city every winter night brings some anonymity and mystique to our life after dark. Walking through to your car in the grocery store parking lot, standing on the corner outside the bar.

If you sit on the levee around early evening, you can watch the fog as it forms like some sort of ancient, ethereal creature. It'll grow several stories tall until the weight of it topples over and the clouds toward you, slowly, like an animal so large it knows nothing can hurt it — quite confident in the fact that it is the strongest thing around.

It's not even that the weather and the natural world are stronger than us, it's how they're other. They don't fight or defeat us, they exist in spite of us. When you crush a roach with your foot, it is incomprehensible to the roach what just appeared and killed it.

Likewise with the fog, the rain, the ways in which the weather and the night control us, despite all our technology and instrumentation. That feeling of eyes on you in the woods, the eerie silence before the tornado siren. The natural world exists in a reality we will not ever understand.

LOCAL WEATHER XIII

What is there to say? The current moment is an infinitely-headed hydra of chaos and despair. There are so many personal hardships, profane statistics, and carpet-bombing judgments ready to lay on a populace made up of ordinary demons and angels and everyone in between. It's exhausting and debilitating.

Yet the animals don't seem to mind. Like a dog on a movie set, the animals can't tell the difference between normal and this. The air feels likewise. The soil. The natural world remains so uncaring and enduring to this unimaginable disaster unfolding. The trees stay standing, the rain still comes.

There's a joke among people right now — what month is it even? But it's not so hard to tell. The air is so hot and humid right now you can't tell if the briny scent is coming from yourself or a warmed-up gust tracked in lazily from the gulf. Downpours in the afternoon — hard and fast — followed by a litany of double texts from the city claiming no responsibility for the damage of the water.

The governor texts us too. And the mayor. And a particularly robotic account that tells us the caseload and death toll every day at high noon, with a note of admonishment or encouragement if the character-count allows. I get these so often I don't read or notice them anymore when they come in, but I wonder if I'll notice when they stop? Or if I'll text STOP before it's all over?

Friday 12:23 PM

NOLAReady: 71 new cases & 0 deaths in NOLA since yesterday. Highest # of cases in one day since Apr. 20. We're very concerned. ready.nola.gov/covid19

Today 1:49 PM

NOLAReady: 63 New Orleanians have been diagnosed with COVID 19 and two have died since yesterday. Do your part to slow the spread & tell a friend!

There's not much I fear more than a loss of control. It used to be that a road trip or airplane was enough to send me into a panic. I often have nightmares of being locked in prison for a crime I'm not sure I committed. Every time I break a bone (I think I'm on nine?), the month or two immobilization of that particular limb pains me more than the pain itself.

That's all to say — when will this end? Optimistically, we're a quarter of the way through, yet I'm already breaking the rules, and I feel like the last to do so. The white people in my neighborhood have been holding get-togethers and parties ever since the studies told us (obviously) that racial privilege still exists in a global health epidemic.

Every time I move to a new place I become more radical in my anarchist belief — something I've believed in longer than anything else. There's something about isolation and loneliness that makes me daydream about how much better society could function.

And now, in this global what-should-be lockdown, the writing is on the wall, in hot pink, digitally-streaming, available-on-all-platform letters so bright I thought it'd burn the retinas of even those with their eyes closed, but the people in power and privilege just continue to refuse the premise itself. There is no writing, there is no wall. Be quiet. You're dividing us. You're making it worse.

And what do you do with that? Especially as a member of this supremely privileged people? I've marched on the interstate, sent texts to my uncle, asked my workplace to fund antiracist training, talked to my therapist, yet it's not enough, and I think that's the point.

Still though, I have to remind myself that this isn't my fault. That capitalism has created all this. That people aren't naturally so awful, ugly, smugly uncaring of their fellow human. But it's become a daily affirmation for me. I need to believe this because otherwise, my Lord. And if it's not true, I'm totally hosed. What's the point in being part of this species if this is who we are?

I just can't believe that this is how people are — despite my long-festering, gangrene suspicion that these people I'm seeing are indeed standard issue models of humanity, no defects present. That there is no them, only us.

I just feel so let down. So hateful. I hate these people who give in to all these toxic, prejudiced ways of thinking because it's easier than just simply *acknowledging* the injustice in the world. I hate that they're the majority (and I'm sick of proving this with Gallup polls). I hate that my really myopic, base level, supremely partial understanding of the world is somehow considered woke.

There are storms every day and, now that I don't leave the house much, it's been nice to open the doors and windows and watch it flood the courtyard for an hour or so every morning or afternoon. I turn off the air conditioner and fans and just listen to it beat down on the plants and the brick. And then the sun comes and in an hour everything is dry — a new freshness in the air.

And as I'm writing all this, people are dying. Some of them I know. And others I know are getting shot at with tear gas and rubber bullets. Thrown in jail. Ostracized from their families for calling out what isn't right, or simply being who they are. And so much else.

Of course, the people in power and privilege still don't care. They've never cared. Intellectually I understand it, but spiritually, I just don't. I just don't get how a person can look at a chart of American COVID cases versus the world, American incarceration rates versus the world, American health outcomes versus the world, and not care.

I don't understand how a person can watch any of the half dozen videos per month of people killed by the police and not find an ounce of care in their bones. The aftermath of a drone strike. An impoverished tent city on the lawn of City Hall.

There's a ticker tape of American violence and failure somewhere and it's spinning impossibly fast, day and night — a de facto perpetual motion device — and the majority of the populace can't smell the motor as it's burning up.

It's enough to drive a good man mad. I think that's why they pretend not to notice. Why they make excuses. That denialism is their panacea.

I still feel so let down. My voice cracked the other day when I said, "I just hate America and I hate white people." I didn't expect such a trite sentence to bring a chill to my arm, but the truth has a way of doing that. Still though, I can't help but feel insane at times, seeing all these people smugly dismiss the humanity of others. Casually accept the deaths of hundreds of thousands.

I know the odds of us winning are impossibly long — but you see, I focus so much on the devil I forget the angels right beside me. I forget where you are and where you chose to sleep tonight. I forget how the gift that is your tenderness, your regard, makes the long-shot of justice something worth betting on. How our shared touch turns simple survival into active resistance.

The air in this room we share is stale and humid, but I'm sharing it with you. Your body on mine is wet with sweat, but it's your sweat, so I don't mind. And I know the virus could take us eventually, but even if it does, it'd need weeks to do its work. That's all to say — it can't take us just yet.

No, we have this morning together, right now, and there's coffee ready on the stove. I'll get it for you, don't move. Just stay there and wait for me.

LOCAL WEATHER XIV

It's tempting to say there's a light at the end of the tunnel, but there's not, just an idea of light. A whisper of blue in the dark. A moment where you're awake and it's still night outside, but your body's not going to let you fall back asleep.

So you get up, walk around, go into the courtyard and stare at the sky. There's a glow in the distance — is it the sunrise, or skyline? The birds somehow know when it's nearly first light, but not me, not people.

I know it's nearly first light only when it seems like night can't last much longer. And then it does. And then it's light.

It's embarrassing to admit how much the adage, "if you're going through hell, keep going" has gotten me through. Or Bruce Lee's cunning, not quite rebuttal to his friend who said that finishing a 5K would kill him, "then die."

I wrote *then die* on my arm when I was hiking a mountain by myself somewhere and didn't think I could finish. We can do things we don't think are possible. We can weather pretty much anything. The trick is believing that enough to take the next step.

When things have been really bad for me, death can even be a little comforting. The knowledge that at least some things are out of my control — the lost will of my parents. That everything ends, so why not? A $5 table when all you've got is $5 — so *come whatever wills all chances.*

But it's not enough to just make it through something. I can't think of a word hotter than *trauma* right now, and it's probably because we're all fucking traumatized beyond comprehension — for obvious and mundane reasons. To finish the line from that Audre Lorde poem, *The stub remains / an ill-pulled tooth with a ragged edge.*

I've made it through a lot. Most people make it through a lot. It's old wisdom that with joy will be strife. Yet the case could also be made that strife is the only thing guaranteed in the world, that not all humans will get joy (billions of other animals are systematically denied it every year).

When Bethanie asks me, *but what did that feel like?*, I have no clue, because really — what does anything feel like? It's a basic question, and I do feel things of course. But I'm not used to examining the feelings. It baffles me that I can be so good at thinking, so bad at feeling.

And I can't help but be scared when things do really move me, and it scares me more that I can't articulate why I'm moved, or what even that movement feels like.

Science tells us there's a response in the nervous system and that your heart rate will rise, palms moisten, breathing quicken — yet what if it doesn't? Because it doesn't. Only the parting of thoughts like a rock in a stream — a catch in the throat — if anything at all. And then it's back to the same old pattern of thought.

It's an affect so intrinsic, so inherent, so a part of me, I can't even tell it's there. A gag that comes with the sudden tasting of bitterness, an animal stalking you through the woods. The birds at dawn.

LOCAL WEATHER XV

It rains for thirty minutes and the alley is underwater again because there's nowhere really for the water to go. The ground's soaked from weeks of rain, the catch basin is full, and downhill isn't a concept that exists for miles.

I've got nowhere to be, but say I do. The first breath away from you calms me quicker than any drug could dare. Each muscle, but especially those that make up the worn wool of my brain, undoes itself and softens. That release of tension where I didn't realize there was tension. A quick crack of the jaw.

I miss you — but those moments together never feel real, and time away from reality takes a toll. It leaves dishes on the counter, both literal and in my head.

It takes work for me to be with you, to be with anyone, in any sense of the word. And yet — I don't think people are meant to be alone. I don't want to be alone. But I do love it more than I should.

Being alone means every moment centers itself around the satiation of your own desire, so what can compete? Like most drugs, it's a hollow joy. I don't want to be alone, but I crave it more than the company of damn near anyone else. I wish it weren't so comfortable to live like this.

I have faith that one day I'll get used to being around someone and that time alone will wear on me instead. That I'll be holed up in a hotel somewhere, counting the days until I'm back home again instead of relishing in the freedom.

When love is done right is when that aloneness grows big enough to encompass the other person in it, where being around that other person becomes so little work that the tradeoff is worth it. I believe this exists. I think it's real. But it's hard to come by. And it's still an unproven theory — the tectonics of loving and sharing time with someone else.

What's more, being alone is just plainly selfish. I truly believe this. It cost money to live like this. It relies on extracted labor, profit, and so on. You're not raising children or caring for the old. To be alone in the world is to be against the world. At least if you're partnered, you have a better shot at making it on your own together. And the fight doesn't feel selfish anymore, but just.

Just as in — the world doesn't want us partnered either. The people in charge want us lonely, separated, and addicted to something — whether it's cane syrup or booze.

Maybe if I trusted you with all this, I'd want you to stay a little longer? If we joined forces — us and our affection against the capitalists and their extraction — the time we spend together wouldn't wear on me so much?

Maybe I'd feel different when I go.

INNATE AFFECTION

It was summer in Missouri, and my friend and I were outside my apartment, both of us barely eighteen, taking a break from the party inside. I had accidentally read something of his I shouldn't have, and had been waiting to ask him about it.

We were smoking Lucky Strikes under a big oak tree by my street, and I asked him if it were true he had cancer. He said he did and that he was dying, would be dead by the spring. He told me not to tell anyone.

The rest of the party passed over me like one long wave of nausea. If I'd read Julia Kristeva by then, I'd have known what I was feeling then was the feeling of abject horror. A sudden, debilitating breakdown between myself and reality, between this new existence and the conception of it I inanely held, just moments ago. I wanted very desperately to unhear what he'd said, as if undoing the moment would undo his prognosis.

It was like my mind was speaking a language my body had forgotten, and its movements for the next hour or so were under the control of something else, a leaf reaching toward the light of a window, cicadas at dusk.

I drank and waited out the party until at last it was just me and my girlfriend, alone in bed. She'd known I had planned on talking to him, and I told her it was true, that he was sick, dying actually, and I let myself collapse into her.

We were still new to sex, new to each other's naked bodies and the ways we could touch — what that touch could do. I cried into her shoulder and she held me, said soothing, forgettable things. I needed her and she was there.

I don't know how it happened, but something about seeing me so sad, so completely destroyed, caused her hands to drift — slowly — from my face to my neck, my neck to my chest, then down a bit more until we were doing something more than simple embrace.

I don't think either of us expected it, to be making love right then, so soon after hearing that our good friend was sick and dying.

I remember feeling strange, even a bit ashamed after, despite it feeling so right in the moment. The slow way she went from listening to holding, from holding to making love. The fact that we fucked and I came.

When people say sex is complicated, they're talking about power. When people say love is stronger than hate, they're refluxing platitudes. I've never cared for either of these ideas — they're banal, at least to me.

But in that moment, in an apartment of my own, with a person I loved more deeply than anyone else, I learned not just the power of love and sex, but the paper walls between them.

I still don't know what made her do that, or think to do that at all. Maybe she was just as blind to her body as I was to my own.

We'd been saying I love you for weeks — initially on accident — but it was what we did with our bodies then that really proved it. I had no idea how love could be as subtle as a scratch, as unconscious as breathing. That this is what a person can do when their lover is aching.

ABOUT THE AUTHOR

Andrew Squitiro is the author of *Local Weather* (Dynamo Verlag, 2023), as well as several chapbooks of poetry from his own press, Gaggle Books. His work has appeared in *Entropy*, *[PANK]*, and *DIAGRAM*, among other journals. He holds an MFA from Old Dominion University and a BA from the University of Missouri. At present, he directs the Office of Undergraduate Research for Tulane University, in New Orleans, where he lives.

DYNAMO VERLAG BOOKS

Telescopes and Other People
JOSH NORMAN

Daughters of Monsters
MELISSA GOODRICH

Peregrine Nation
LUCIAN MATTISON

The Much Love Sad Dawg Trio
MATTHEW SADLER

Driving Around, Looking in Other People's Windows
CL BLEDSOE

Star Things
JESS L PARKER

On Ruben Slikk
CALEB TRUE

Local Weather
ANDREW SQUITIRO

A Human Moon
ALLELIAH NUGUID

DYNAMOVERLAG.COM

www.ingramcontent.com/pod-product-compliance
Lightning Source LLC
Chambersburg PA
CBHW031308120726
47906CB00003B/947

* 9 7 8 1 0 8 8 2 1 4 7 3 2 *